Self-Publish Books and E-Books in India: A Guide to Self-Publishing

By Siva Prasad Bose and Joy Bose

Self Publish Books and e-Books in India

Siva Prasad Bose and Joy Bose

Published by Joy Bose, 2022.

Contents

Dedication

This book is dedicated to all authors and publishers who are involved in the self-publishing industry in India.

Acknowledgements

The authors would like to thank all the wonderful web based platforms available today that make it easier for self published authors to prepare and design their manuscript, including Amazon KDP, IngramSpark, Draft2Digital, Smashwords, Notion Press, Pothi and others.

Also, we would like to acknowledge and thank sites such as Canva that help in designing great book covers, sites like reedsy,com that help to format the book beautifully, free online sites for making diagrams such as draw.io, animation software such as doodly and book readers sites such as goodreads. All these tools make it much easier for first time authors to create better books for readers.

Preface

In recent years, self-publishing has become an increasingly viable and attractive option for authors, particularly in countries like India. With the growing availability of digital tools and online publishing platforms, many authors are choosing to take the self-publishing route instead of going through traditional publishing channels. This approach allows for lower upfront costs, greater control over the publishing process, and quicker time to market.

This book serves as a practical guide for aspiring authors in India who wish to self-publish their work. It covers the end-to-end process, from writing and formatting a manuscript to publishing it in various formats, including eBooks, paperbacks, and audiobooks. Additionally, the book discusses tools, software, and platforms that are suitable for Indian authors, including those who write in Indian languages.

We have also included specific information on the challenges Indian authors may face, such as limited language support in global platforms and how to work around them. There are dedicated chapters on marketing and promoting self-published books, as well as suggestions for low-cost tools and services that first-time authors may find helpful. This updated edition also covers the use of AI writing tools such as ChatGPT, Google

Gemini, and Claude, which have become significant aids for authors in recent years, as well as new marketing strategies such as BookTok and email newsletters.

It is hoped that this book will provide new authors, especially those based in India or writing in Indian languages, with a clear roadmap to begin their self-publishing journey with confidence.

Chapter 1: Why go for Self-Publishing?

Self-publishing is a way for new authors to publish their books with minimal costs and reasonable investments in time and effort and get them out to the readers as soon as they wish. Instead of approaching a traditional publisher with their manuscript, self-publishing means that the authors themselves bear the burden of formatting and editing their books, designing the cover and so on. In some cases, self-publishing also includes the marketing and publicity for the published books.

In this chapter, we discuss the pros and cons of self-publishing as compared to traditional book publishing and hybrid publishing. We examine why self-publishing has become an increasingly popular choice among authors. Understanding its advantages, limitations, and how it compares to traditional and hybrid methods will help you make an informed choice suitable for your goals.

1.1 Traditional Book Publishing Process

In traditional publishing, the author has to send extracts of their manuscripts, such as a hundred pages or a few chapters, to various established publishers for consideration. The establishing publishing houses then decide, based on the projected sales and other criteria, whether to accept or reject the book for publication.

Another way to traditional publishing is the following: A few authors, or members of the public, are invited by the publishers to submit their manuscripts on specific topics. The publishers then examine the submitted manuscripts by the authors and decide whether to accept or reject the book for publication.

If the manuscript is accepted for publishing, the authors sign a contract with the publishers to complete their book within a mutually agreed timeline. As part of the contract, they usually get a fee from the publishers for completing the book, as well as a share of the royalties from the sales of the book.

The publishers, who are usually well-known book companies that publish thousands of books every year, then take the responsibility of designing the layout and cover, printing, marketing and selling the book through various channels. They may also assist the author with proofreading, illustrations and guidance for writing a more readable book that the intended audience would like to read. They usually have dedicated professional teams for each of these tasks.

Sometimes, professional publishing agents or literary agencies act as the middlemen between the authors and the traditional publishers. They do the work of proofreading the book and marketing it to the publishers, and receive a fee which might be a percentage of the royalties from book sales. Some famous literary agents in India include Writer's Side, Red Ink Literary Agency, Siyahi, Jacaranda and Lotus Lane.

1.2 Pros and Cons of Traditional Publishing

The advantages of traditional publishing include the following:

- The author may get professional help and guidance in writing the book and steps such as proof reading and editing.
- The author does not have to worry about the formatting and design for their book.
- The steps for marketing and selling the book are all handled by the publisher, so the author does not need to worry about these steps either.
- The books sold via traditional publishers are more likely to reach a wider audience, since they might already have relationships with various bookstores and distribution channels such as book fairs. They might also have well defined procedures for book promotion and advertising for the books. They also might include the books in their catalogues, where potential buyers can find out about the books.
- The retail cost of the books sold by traditional publishers might be lower, due to economies of scale. This may result in more copies sold and higher royalties for the author.
- The traditional publishers, if they accept to publish the book, would typically cover all costs for editing, marketing, and other steps, and also pay royalties to the author as per the publishing contract.

The disadvantages of using traditional publishers include the following:

- The author is often not in control of important decisions related to their book, such as design and content and the audience to whom the book is marketed.

- It is difficult for new authors to get their books accepted by an established publishing house. Often, such publishers may not even accept submissions by new and unknown authors and only rely on invited and known authors, or established literary agents.

- The authors might not get paid adequately, especially if the publishing houses do not disclose the full volume of the book sales. In addition, the publishers typically take a larger share of the sale price of the book than in case of self-publishing.

1.3 The Self-Publishing Process

In self-publishing, the author typically controls all the stages of the book writing and publishing process. They first type their manuscript draft using any word processing software such as Microsoft word.

After the draft is prepared, the author usually proof-read their own manuscripts or get it done by their friends or contacts. The authors then use available software, including web-based tools, to format their book in a commonly used format for ebooks such as epub or pdf or kindle format.

Alternatively, an author can use paid editing services from freelancing platforms such as reedsy.com and fiverr.com to get their manuscript edited and designed by professionals. It is usually cheaper to pay for individual services such as editing and proofreading and cover design at freelancing platforms, than to take an assisted book publication package.

Once the book is completed and prepared in the correct format, the authors then upload the book using the web-based interfaces provided by companies that offer self-publishing in online platforms, such as Amazon KDP or Draft2Digital or Smashwords or IngramSpark. After a few checks of the uploaded book draft by the online platform, which may be automated, the book is then published.

The marketing of the published book and reaching out to potential readers is usually also the responsibility of the authors, via blogs, book readings and so on.

1.4 Pros and Cons of Self-Publishing

The advantages of self-publishing are as follows:

- It is often quicker for an author to self-publish a book, given the range of tools and platforms available.
- The author does not need to pass through a vetting process by the publisher
- The author has freedom to use whichever tools, formats, software and companies they like in order to publish the book.
- The entire royalties from the sales, apart from the publisher's cut, go straight to the author. The royalties are usually in the range of 30-70% of the sale price.
- The author can add on additional services such as editing and designing, as per their needs, in a pay-as-

you-go way, while also maintaining full control of the book sales and royalties.

The disadvantages are:

- There is work involved for the author to format and market their book.
- The author may not be an expert in cover design and so on.
- The marketing may also be the responsibility of the author and they might not have the needed skills to market their book to potential buyers.
- The audience for self-published books is limited.
- It is more difficult for new readers to discover self-published books, in the absence of targeted promotions by the publishers.
- While many of the self-publishing services such as Draft2Digital and Amazon KDP are free, some of them are not free and could result in costs for authors that they would be unable to recoup in book sales.
- There may be vanity publishers who charge authors an unreasonably large fee for self-publishing their books. Their value-add services, if any, might not be worth the amount of fees they charge from the authors.

1.5 Costs of Self-Publishing

If the author only uses the available online web-based tools and does not take any assistance in proofreading, design and marketing the book, the cost of self-publishing can be free in many online platforms.

If the author chooses to take assistance of the self-publishing companies for some or all aspects of the design and marketing, their costs will correspondingly increase.

Many of the companies now offer packages to the author based on the levels of service they require. The cost could vary from a few thousands of rupees to tens of thousands, depending on various factors. They include the following:

- Choice of publisher and platform.
- Whether it is a hard copy (paperback or hardback) or e-book or audio book.
- Whether the author does all the steps themselves or outsources some of the steps to the publisher.

For example, Notion Press, a well-known self-publishing company in India, has packages that vary from to free to Rs 4990 to 35990 plus GST tax to help with the various steps of publishing the books.

1.6 Hybrid Publishing

Hybrid publishing, also sometimes called assisted self-publishing, mixes elements from traditional and self-publishing. They charge the authors a set fee for a bundle of services such as editing, designing and formatting, marketing, etc. for a book. They may have different packages of services offered at different set prices, and work closely with the authors from the book conceptualization stage, aiming to improve the quality of the finished book in this way. The authors can take advantage of available experts in domains such as book design and editing. The hybrid publishers themselves take charge of all sales and distribution for the books, and pay the authors royalties as an agreed percentage of the sales.

However, their value-add for the amount charged to the authors can vary and some authors may be reluctant to give up control of aspects of their book design, publication and distribution. In addition, some of the publishers may not pay the full royalties due to the authors in a timely way. Also, many authors may not be able to recoup their initial investment in the offered publishing packages by way of book sales.

1.7 Conclusion

In this chapter, we explored the benefits and challenges of self-publishing compared to traditional and hybrid methods. Understanding these distinctions helps authors make informed decisions. In the next chapter, we move forward by planning how you can systematically approach writing your book.

Chapter 2: Tips to Plan to Write a Book

With clarity about self-publishing, the next essential step is planning your book-writing process. In this chapter, we discuss a few tips and techniques that an author can use to systematically approach writing, ensuring efficiency, productivity, and sustained motivation.

2.1 Break the book into manageable chunks

Writing a book can seem a hard task at first and can be deterring to first time authors. The trick is to break it down into manageable chunks.

Writing a book may be motivated by a new author's interest or as a hobby. Seen in that way, they may treat it as a pleasure task to be completed at their leisure. However, it is sometimes better to treat the task of book writing as a project, with proper planning and timelines for completion of various stages of the book.

Therefore, the author can use project management tools, such as Gantt charts, Microsoft project, Kanban, or Jira boards, to execute the book writing project.

Figure: Executing a project using a Kanban board. Photo by Jo Szczepanska on Unsplash

The timeline for completing the book can be 3-6 months or one or more years, depending on the author's available time, the proposed length of the book and the author's speed of writing. Whatever be the timeline based on the time the author can spare, it is good to try and stick to it. This may be difficult in cases where the author has some other full time or part time jobs, and have to essentially motivate themselves in the absence of a manager.

2.2 Write the book outline first

For a new author to properly plan the book, they should write the outline of their book first: the title, chapters and subsections in each chapter.

```
Book outline
Table of contents

Preface
Chapter 1. Introduction
Chapter 2.
Chapter 3.
Chapter 4.
Chapter 5. Conclusion
```

Figure: A sample book outline

Writing the outline at the onset before starting to write the book content will force the author to think carefully about what message they want the readers to take away and how their book will build on the ideas. This is applicable for both fiction and non-fiction books, but particularly for non-fiction.

While writing the outline, it may also be useful to think a little bit about the intended audience and how the book may be useful to them and what kind of book they would write to read. One can see other books of the same genre to get some guidance in this matter.

2.3 Write something every day

Procrastination and laziness are the bane of any book author. Also, one of the famous problems for writers is called "writer's block", where the author is stuck in the middle of the writing and unable to produce anything at all for their book.

In order to combat these, one useful strategy is to write a little bit, even as less as a few sentences or paragraph, every single day, rather than write in big chunks in a single sitting. This is inspired by a Japanese technique called kaizen, which means to take a few steps every day towards the eventual goal. This technique can give a feeling of achievement and help to combat writer's block and procrastination to a large extent.

2.4 Type or hand write the book

The author can decide whether to type the whole book on a computer, or to write it by hand first and then type it later, or a mixture of the two. Different authors have different styles, and there is no one style that is perfect.

However, typing on a computer can enable the author to take advantage of the tools such as spelling and grammar checkers that are available.

Grammarly (https://www.grammarly.com/) is one such useful AI-enabled tool to flag and suggest corrections to grammatical errors in a manuscript.

Microsoft Word's autocorrect can also be a useful tool for spell checks and grammar checks.

Figure: Spelling and grammar check in Microsoft Word

2.5 Visualize the completed book

To motivate the author, one tool that can be useful is to visualize how the book might look like once it is completed, and how the reader will feel when they are reading the book. They can visualize their target reader reading the completed book and enjoying reading it. This kind of visualization can serve as a good motivation to finish the book and to deal with any psychological blockers for their productivity.

2.6 Complete the book in iterations

Some authors may find it useful to finish a book in iterations. This means to get out a first draft of the whole book as soon as possible, then read and make corrections to improve the draft, and repeat the process multiple times for subsequent drafts, until they are happy with the final draft version of the book. This way, the completed draft shall many editing and other errors already corrected.

Other authors may find it useful to do this improvement and iterations chapter by chapter, rather than for the whole book. This means writing one chapter, carefully going through the draft of the chapter or sharing with their friends for feedback. Only when the author is happy with the completed chapter, they start writing the next one.

In these days of self-publishing, one could even do the publishing of the book edition by edition, which is similar to iterations but on a longer timescale.

Figure: Some good books to learn about writing

2.7 Some good books for writing

Following are a few good books to improve writing skills for budding authors:

- **On Writing Well: The Classic Guide to Writing Nonfiction by William Zinsser.** URL: https://www.goodreads.com/book/show/ 53343.On_Writing_Well This book has good advice for writing non fiction, with general tips about methods and principles on good writing and how to write a good travel article, interview memoir etc. It is useful for non fiction writers.
- **On Writing: A Memoir of the Craft by Stephen King.** URL: https://www.goodreads.com/book/ show/10569.On_Writing This book is by the famous author and novelist Stephen King. It is written in a very lucid style. King states his own experiences on how he started writing and different experiences that inspired him to write.
- **The Elements of Style by William Strunk Jr., E.B. White.** URL: https://www.goodreads.com/book/ show/33514.The_Elements_of_Style This book contains extremely useful advice about writing styles, and is indispensable for good writing.

2.8 Using AI Tools to Assist in Writing

In recent years, Artificial Intelligence (AI) tools have become widely available and can be a significant aid to authors in the writing process. These tools use large language models (LLMs) trained on vast amounts of text to assist with brainstorming, drafting, editing, and more. It is important to note that AI tools should be used to augment an author's creativity, not replace it. The final voice, ideas, and content decisions should always remain with the human author.

Some of the most popular AI tools that authors can use include the following:

- **ChatGPT (https://chat.openai.com/):** Developed by OpenAI, ChatGPT is one of the most widely used AI tools for authors. It can help with brainstorming story ideas, generating dialogue, drafting sections of a book, and rewriting text in a different style or tone. A free tier is available, and a paid subscription (GPT Plus) offers access to more advanced models. It is a particularly strong all-round tool for both fiction and non-fiction writing.
- **Google Gemini (https://gemini.google.com/):** Google's AI assistant is particularly strong for research tasks, fact-checking, and writing accuracy-focused non-fiction. Because it is integrated with Google's ecosystem, it can draw on up-to-date information from the web. It is useful for authors who need to verify information or generate well-structured outlines for educational or non-fiction books.
- **Claude (https://claude.ai/):** Developed by Anthropic, Claude is particularly praised for crafting natural-sounding dialogue and developing character voice. It handles long documents well and can assist with editing, proofreading, and providing detailed

feedback on a manuscript. Authors appreciate its thoughtful and nuanced responses.

- **Grammarly (https://www.grammarly.com/):** This AI-powered writing assistant goes beyond basic spell-checking to offer grammar corrections, style suggestions, tone adjustments, and clarity improvements. It integrates directly into word processors and browsers, making it easy to use during the writing and editing process. A free tier is available, with a premium version offering more advanced features.

Authors should be aware that most book publishers and online retailers currently require authors to disclose if significant portions of their book were generated by AI. It is always advisable to check the policies of the publishing platform before using AI-generated content in a book intended for commercial sale. AI tools work best when used for research, inspiration, editing feedback, and overcoming writer's block — rather than for wholesale generation of the book's content.

2.9 Conclusion

In this chapter, we discussed practical strategies to break down the intimidating task of writing into manageable steps, combat procrastination, and maintain motivation. With your manuscript prepared, the next critical step is formatting your book professionally, which we will cover in the next chapter.

Chapter 3: Ways to Format a Book

Once you have completed your manuscript, professional formatting becomes crucial. A well formatted book is pleasing to the reader's eye, leading to a better reading experience and also better sales for the authors. Therefore, it is important to pay attention to the formatting and if needed, invest time and money in getting the book properly formatted.

In this chapter, we introduce various tools and practices to make your book visually appealing and reader-friendly, significantly enhancing its marketability.

3.1 Sections in a book

A book can have the following main sections:

- Cover Page
- Table of contents
- (Optional sections) Acknowledgements, Dedication, Copyright
- Preface
- Chapters of the book
- Chapter 1: Title
- Chapter 2: Title
- ... (Chapter n) Title
- (Optional section) Glossary
- (Optional section) Other books by the same author

An author can plan to structure their book with similar sections. However, there is no hard and fast rule about this, and variations are quite possible.

A Microsoft Word document with these sections can serve as a good starting point or template for writing a book. It is a good idea to have some idea of the approximate structure in mind, as to how the topics (in case of a non-fiction book) or storyline (in case of a fiction book) will be developed.

3.2 Which format to use to write a book manuscript

Microsoft Word is an easy starting choice for writing a book. Its intuitive interface, in-built spell and grammar checking, and widespread popularity are important advantages. There are also many online tools available to convert Word documents including doc and docx files into other formats such as PDF.

However, for publishing e-books, using Microsoft Word may not always work, since different E-book readers might accept books in different formats. So, the author would either need to write the book in such formats as are needed by the publishing platform, or else convert the book, written originally in MS Word, into these formats.

For E-books, it makes more sense to use a format that is compatible across multiple different e-book readers. EPUB is the most widely used format for this purpose.

Also, for compatibility reasons across different formats, it is good to write a book in a simple format with as less formatting as possible. The reason for this is that too much formatting introduces hidden markup characters in the file, which can cause a problem when converting to different formats. Hence, writing the text in a format-less editor such as notepad or as HTML may not be a bad idea. Images, if any, can be inserted on top of the minimally formatted manuscript.

With less formatting and hidden markup, we will get the most accurate idea of how our completed eBook will look on different kinds of devices and e-readers.

Some popular file formats for writing e-books are as follows:

- **EPUB**: It is an industry standard for EBooks and is compatible with most publishers such as Apple books, Smashwords, Google play, Draft2Digital, Amazon Kindle and others. One could create an epub file by converting from formats like MS Word or using some web-based tools like the converter available with Draft2Digital (https://www.draft2digital.com/)

Books written in EPUB format can be read using free EPUB readers such as Icecream EBook reader, Freda and Calibre.

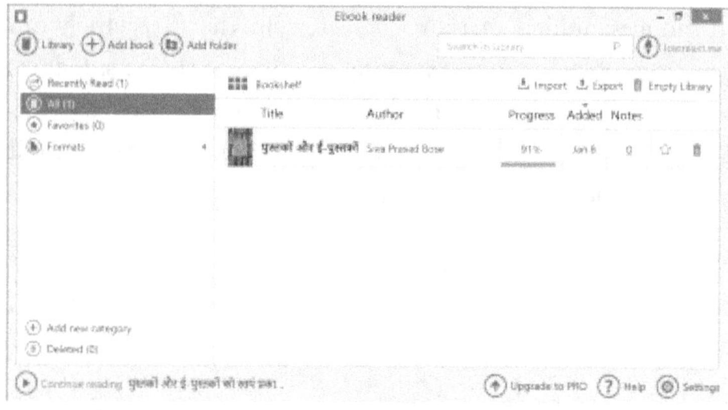

Figure: Interface of Icecream EBook Reader

- **Mobi**: This format is meant mainly for e-books and paperbacks published by Amazon Kindle Direct Publishing (KDP, https://kdp.amazon.com/en_US/) and compatible on Amazon Kindle and a few other Ebook readers. Here too, one can convert from MS Word using software such as Kindle Create, which can be downloaded from the amazon.com website. Recently, Amazon kindle has been encouraging use of the Kindle create software for books uploaded on amazon KDP, so the use of MOBI format is decreasing.

- **Word processing software such as Microsoft Word**: Word (and similar word processing software such as OpenOffice, Google docs and Apple Pages) is one of the most popular and easiest formats to write any document. It also has tools such as spell checkers built into it.

- **PDF (Portable Document Format)**: The PDF

format is easy to print and works across platforms. Books written in word processing software such as Microsoft Word may easily be converted to PDF by "Save As" function on Microsoft Word. These books may directly be compatible with some publishers such as Google play books. Or else, such books can be easily converted into Amazon kindle and other formats using their respective software such as Amazon KDP.

For their chosen format, the author can use web-based software or any other software to write the books. There are many free book publishing tools available on Windows, Linux and Mac platforms, as well as web-based tools such as Google docs. Also, most book publishers and e-book publishers usually have their own online tools or converters that an author can use to compose their books.

3.3 Testing how the finished book looks in different formats and mediums

Once a book is composed in a specific format, it is important to view how the finished book looks like in in different formats and mediums.

Sometimes, language specific fonts, images, equations and other items may not come out properly when the format is converted, such as Microsoft Word to EPUB. That is why it is important to view how the finished book looks like in different formats before submitting for publication. Another option for an author is to create multiple versions of their book, each for a different format.

Along with viewing the book in different formats, one should also view the finished book in different devices with different form factors and e-readers. Such devices can include the following:

- Kindle
- iPod
- Nook
- PC app
- Mobile phone

For example, the Amazon KDP software allows authors to view their finished book from the Kindle app, web based app, mobile phone and amazon kindle device.

Figure: Interface of the Canva online Ebook Maker

There are also specialized online companies that have online software for designing beautiful looking books. A notable example is Canva Book Maker (https://www.canva.com/create/ebooks/) which has a number of beautiful templates to design E-Books.

3.4 Free book publishing tools that authors can use

In this subsection we discuss a few good and freely available tools that authors can use to publish their books.

Kindle create is one of the good software that is meant for publishing using Amazon KDP. It needs to be downloaded from the Amazon website and installed on the PC or Mac. It is mainly meant for the books that the author intends to publish for Amazon kindle.

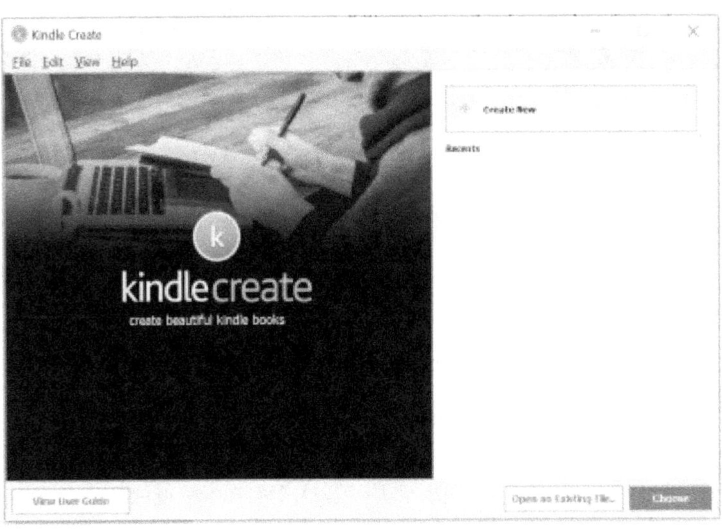

Figure: Installing the Kindle create software from the Amazon website

The author can import the book as a word file into kindle create, which will do all the formatting in a way that is suitable for kindle, as well as detect and insert a table of contents for the book. However, sometimes there may be minor mismatches in chapter headings and formatting, so the author is advised to manually check each page if it is to their satisfaction.

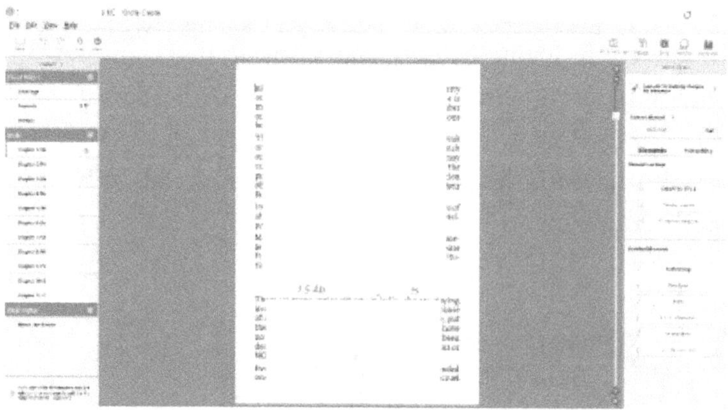

Figure: Composing a book using Kindle create software on a PC

Apple Macs have the Apple Pages software (https://support.apple.com/en-us/HT208499) that can be used to compose beautiful looking books. The books created using the Pages software are compatible with Apple Books and others. The composed books using Apple pages are convertible to EPUB format that is compatible with all major book readers.

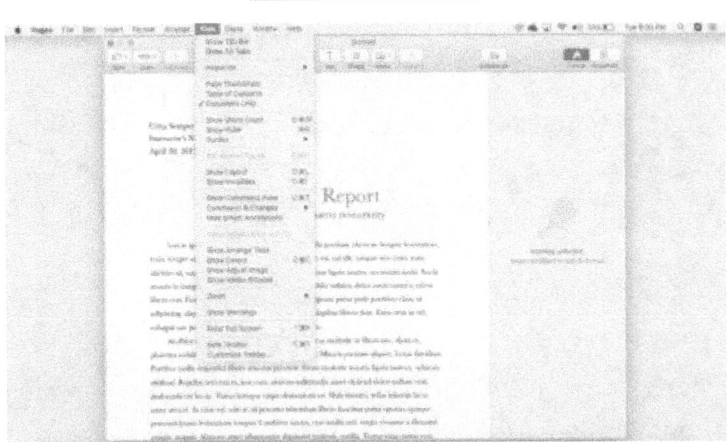

Figure: Interface of the Apple Pages software for composing books on a Mac

3.5 Adding illustrations, diagrams, and flowcharts

Adding visual elements such as flowcharts, illustrations and diagrams greatly enhances the readability and readers' interest in the book.

For adding diagrams and illustrations, authors can use various software such as draw.io online tool for diagrams and flowcharts, Microsoft Powerpoint, Microsoft Visio and others. Most of the online software such as draw.io are available for free, although there might be paid software such as Adobe Photoshop that have more or better features.

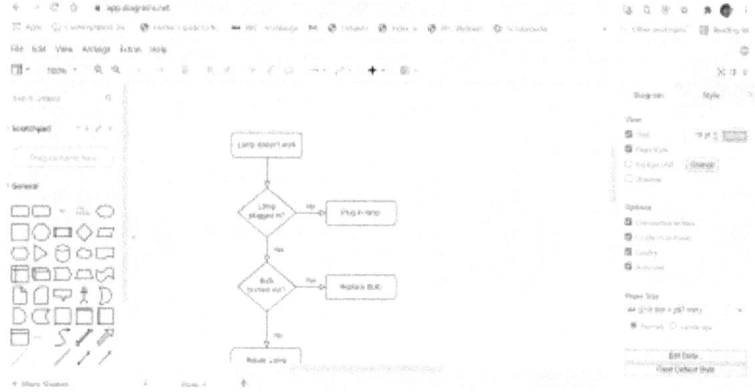

Figure: Interface of the draw.io free online software for composing flowcharts and illustrations.

3.6 Designing a cover for the book

The cover is the first part of the book that readers get to see. Therefore, it is important to have a professional looking cover to entice readers to buy the book.

Canva.com is one of the good websites where one can design professional looking book covers. It provides a lot of templates, including both free and paid templates. If the author chooses to pay, the range of available templates and relevant images for designing the cover is much wider.

Many other such online websites for designing book covers are also available.

Amazon KDP and other publishers also usually provide a cover designer tool.

The cover designer software may have a collection of templates for book covers in various genres such as fiction book, non-fiction, or autobiography. In addition, they may have a collection of paid and free images for various keywords. There would be a way to customize the images in the templates by using drag and drop, or to change the color scheme, font and so on.

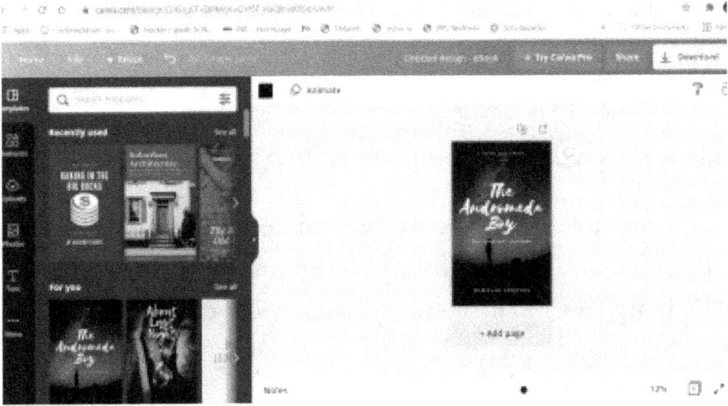

Figure: Canva.com web-based interface for designing book covers

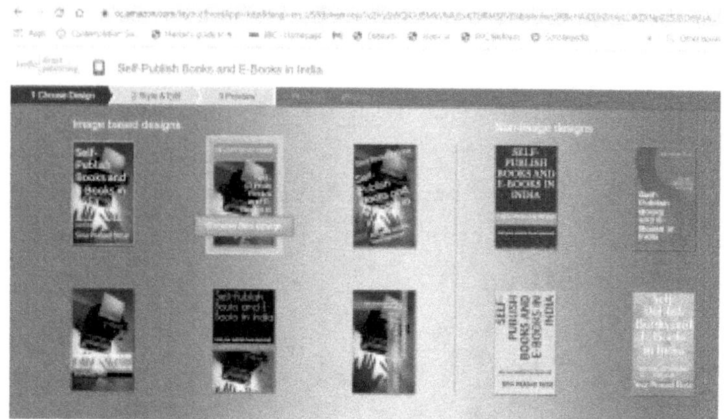

Figure: Interface of the Amazon KDP cover creator

However, in choosing templates and designs for book covers, the choice of free designs and images might be limited. The paid templates and images may have a wider range and a higher number of high-quality images.

3.7 Conclusion

In this chapter, we have surveyed a few popular tools, including both web based and downloadable software, that are available for authors to format and design their books. While these are no means the only tools available, new authors can use these as a starting point for designing their books, so that they appear professional and appealing for readers.

Having formatted your manuscript, in the next chapter we will explore how to effectively publish your e-book on various platforms.

Chapter 4: How to publish E-books

Having formatted your manuscript, your next step is to make it accessible to readers worldwide. In this chapter, we explore various digital platforms and practical steps to successfully publish your e-book, maximizing your online presence and audience reach.

Nowadays there are multiple e-book publishers available to authors from all over the world. Most of them allow e-book publishing for free or at a nominal price. Some of them provide tools for formatting. A few publishers provide additional services like marketing as well.

4.1 Kindle Direct Publishing (KDP)

Amazon has the biggest reach of any bookstore in the world, so it should be the first choice of any author. The market share of amazon varies from 40% to 80% in most countries. Amazon has got a very good interface using a web based platform called kindle direct publishing or KDP to create e-books (for distribution in Kindle) and print books. Recently, they have even added the facility for authors to design hardcover editions for their book, provided it has a minimum number of pages (usually 75 pages).

Figure: Interface of Amazon KDP for adding a new book

The KDP website is at https://kdp.amazon.com/en_US/

An author can create their books using the Kindle create software mentioned in the previous chapter, which saves the completed book as a KPF file.

Alternatively, the authors can write the books using Microsoft Word or any of the other popular formats like EPUB.

Once ready, the book file can be uploaded to the KDP website. The interface also needs a few more details such as book title, genre, language, author details, book summary, selling price etc.

The online interface of KDP then performs a few checks. It has options for the author to design a cover using KDP's cover creator software or upload their own cover designed externally, such as by using Canva.com.

Once all this is done, the finished book can be previewed using the same KDP interface. For e-books on kindle, the author can view how it looks on different devices such as tablet, desktop, mobile phone and kindle reader. Once the author approves the preview, the e-book is then published on amazon.

One can also use KDP Select to promote their book by enrolling it as part of the kindle unlimited program, where kindle unlimited members can access and read the books, and authors get paid on the basis of number of pages read.

However it must be noted that KDP select is exclusive to amazon, meaning that an author must not put their e-books on any other platform when using KDP select (print books are fine and can be put on other platforms). The author can decide the price of the book as well as the revenue split. Amazon also has an "expanded distribution" option for USA and UK markets where the revenue shared with the author is lower but the opportunity is available to sell the book on a higher number of external retailers.

4.2 Google play books

In order to list or sell their books on Google play books, an author can create the word file or PDF file of the book and upload it on google play, using the google play books partner center.

The main advantage of listing one's book on google play and google books is that it is more likely to appear higher in google searches.

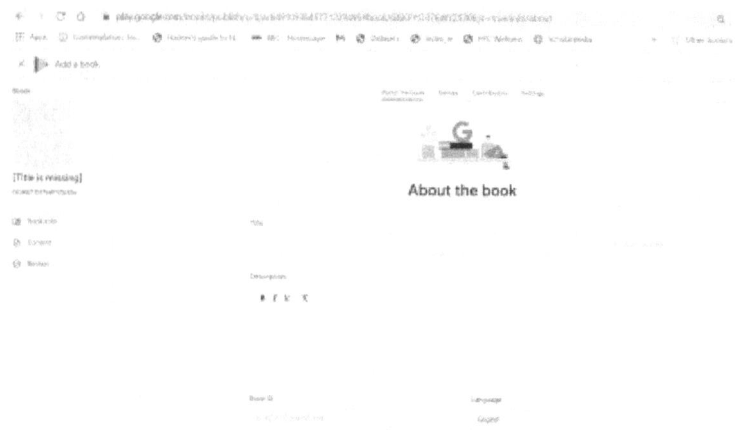

Figure: Interface of Google play books partner center for adding details of a new book

The website URL of the Google play partner center is https://play.google.com/books/publish/u/0/

The author has to first go to the website, fill the basic details and then upload the files for the book such as the cover and the content.

Once the book cover and interior PDF files are added using the interface, it will get listed as part of the google play books. Here, the author can choose one of the following two actions:

- List the book for sale (after specifying the book price in different countries) on Google Play.
- List the book for preview on Google Books. The means putting a few pages (say 10-20% of the book) for people to read and google search to index the book.

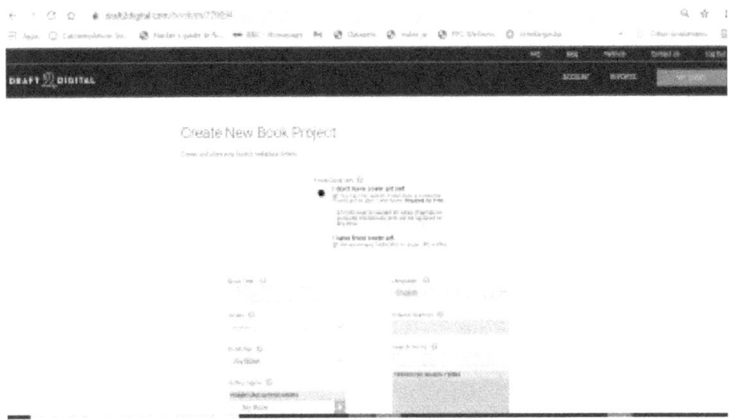

Figure: Interface of draft2digital webpage (https://www.draft2digital.com/) for adding details of a new book. Once ready, the e-book is then distributed to different publishers.

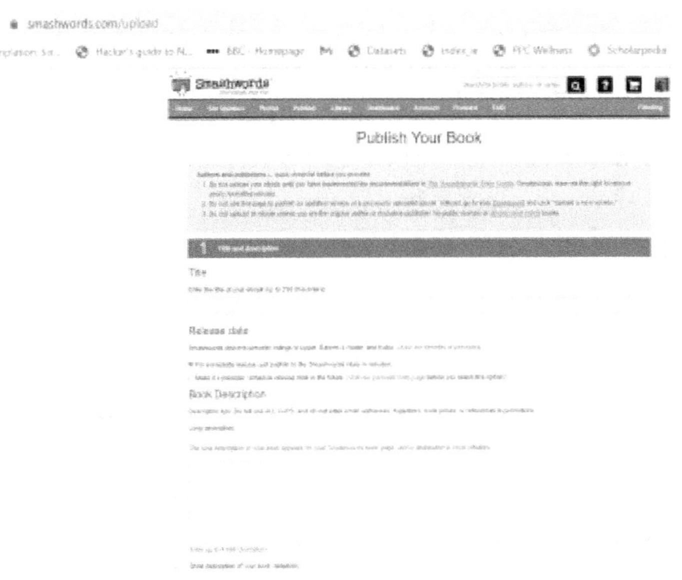

Figure: Interface of the Smashwords website (https://www.smashwords.com/) for adding details of a new book.

4.3 Draft2Digital and Smashwords

Draft2digital (https://www.draft2digital.com/) is an excellent free site which can distribute created e-books to multiple sites such as Rakuten Kobo, Barnes and Noble, Apple Books, Scribd, Bibliotheca etc.

Using Draft2Digital can save the book author a lot of time and effort in distributing their e-books to multiple publishing sites. The author can decide a single price worldwide for their books or different prices for different publishers.

Using the online Draft2Digital interface, one can add details of a new book. One can upload the book manuscript in any common format such as PDF or DOC or EPUB, and the web-based interface converts it to EPUB. The author has the chance to look at the finished EPUB version and correct any errors. Once the author has approved the final version, it is made available by Draft2Digital for distribution to various online publishers. The process of distribution is amazingly quick, taking only a few hours for some publishers to a few days at most for others.

Smashwords (https://www.smashwords.com/) is another popular online website for creating and distributing e-books to various publishers. It is similar to Draft2Digital in that the author has to upload one file of the book manuscript and Smashwords will distribute it to multiple publishers. They have a style guide to which the authors must conform before their book is approved for "Premium Status" making it eligible for distribution to external retailers.

Draft2Digital completed its acquisition of Smashwords in 2022, and by 2025 the full migration of all Smashwords author accounts into the Draft2Digital platform was complete. Authors who previously published through Smashwords now manage their books through the Draft2Digital dashboard. The Smashwords brand continues to operate as a reader-facing bookstore (smashwords.com), while all publishing and distribution functions are now handled through Draft2Digital. Authors benefit from the combined distribution reach of both companies, and can access Smashwords marketing tools such as coupon promotions and storewide sales through their Draft2Digital account.

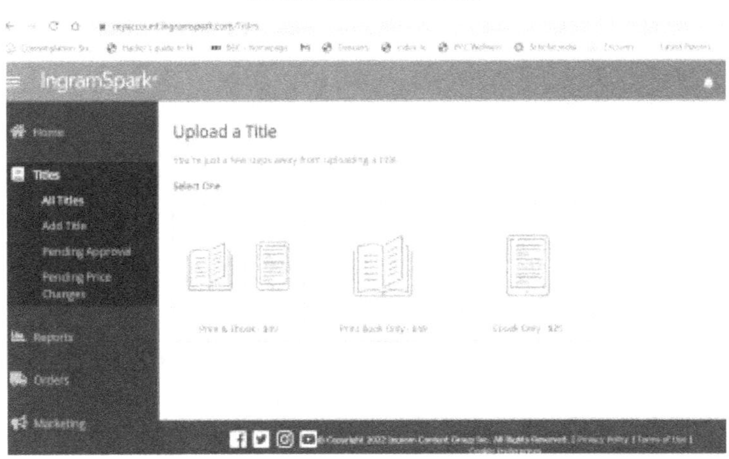

Figure: Interface of IngramSpark app for uploading a new book

4.4 IngramSpark

IngramSpark is a very popular publisher for paperback and hardback books targeted to bookstores, rather than eBooks. They charge a fixed price for each book that is uploaded and published by them, to be paid by the author. The price is usually $25 for eboks and $49 for print and ebooks combined. The author can use their web tools for designing the book. They have possibly the widest distribution reach for the US market.

However, IngramSpark do not provide an ISBN number for non-US authors. Therefore, authors based in India and other countries must get their own ISBN. For India, the ISBNs can be obtained from the Raja Rammohun Roy National Agency for ISBN using their website whose URL is https://isbn.gov.in/.

4.5 Other publishers

Similar to Draft2Digital and Smashwords, there are a number of other worldwide publishers that can distribute E-books to different sites.

Some of them are as follows:

- Apple books for authors https://authors.apple.com/
- IngramSpark https://www.ingramspark.com/
- Lulu https://www.lulu.com/
- Kobo Writing Life https://www.kobo.com/us/en/p/writinglife

- Barnes and Noble https://press.barnesandnoble.com/

There are also a few country or region specific publishers such as:

- e-Sentral for South East Asia https://publisher.e-sentral.com/
- Bookrix for Germany and Europe https://www.bookrix.com/

4.6 India specific publishers for E-books

Some India specific self-publishing companies for E-books include the following:

- Pothi.com https://pothi.com/ : Pothi.com also publishes ebooks as PDFs.
- NotionPress https://www.notionpress.com/ : NotionPress has recently started publishing ebooks in addition to as print books.
- Pencil https://www.thepencilapp.com/

There are also other Indian companies for e-books that an author may search on Google and use.

One advantage of using India specific companies is that they would have better support for Indian languages like Hindi, Bengali, Tamil, Marathi etc. Also, their pricing and services would be tailored for the Indian market.

4.7 Choosing whether to go wide or be exclusive to amazon

For any new author, they need to decide whether to stick exclusively with Amazon and enroll in Amazon's KDP Select program or "go wide" and distribute their book to multiple retailers such as Draft2Digital and IngramSpark.

There are pros and cons of both the options. The advantages of sticking exclusively with Amazon KDP Select are as follows:

- Amazon offers the author the chance to promote their book for free or at special discounts.
- The discounts and free books are publicized separately so potential buyers looking for cheap deals can find them easily.
- Those Amazon subscribers who have kindle unlimited subscription can read your book for free, and the author gets some royalty for each page read.
- KDP Select offers a new and unknown author the chance to get a good readership for their first books by offering them for free or at a discount. Once they have built a readership, they can then price their subsequent books at a higher price.
- Since Amazon controls upto 80% of the books and ebooks market in many countries, going exclusively with amazon means the author has a better chance of reaching more potential customers. However the author should check what is the number for their own country before making any final decision.

The disadvantages to an author of going exclusively with KDP Select are as follows:

- Ebooks enrolled in Amazon's KDP select cannot be distributed to other competing eBook publishers such as Draft2Digital or Google play books. This can limit the range of customers the author wants to reach.
- In some countries, the market share of Amazon is not that high. For those countries, a new author may be able to reach more customers by distributing their books to as many distributors as possible, rather than sticking exclusively with amazon.

Some authors may choose to go hybrid i.e., enroll their book exclusively with Amazon KDP select for three months (which is the minimum exclusive time), then take the book out of KDP select and distribute it with all other publishers such as Draft2Digital. In a way, this strategy can enable the author to get the best of both worlds.

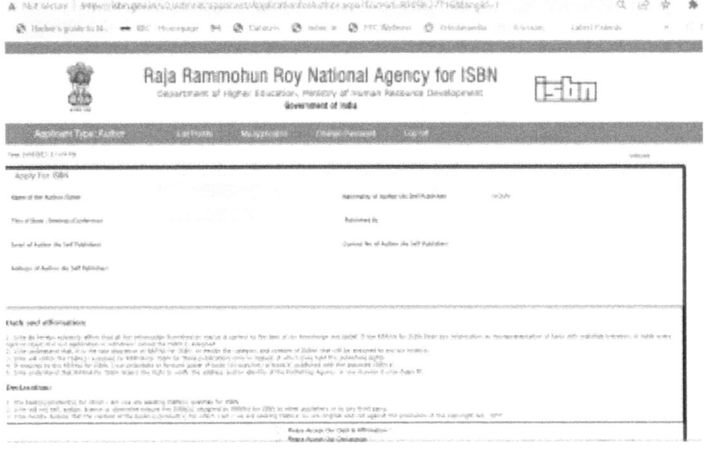

Figure: Interface of the Indian National Agency for ISBN for adding details of a new book to get ISBN numbers

4.8 Free ISBNs

An important issue to keep in mind is the availability of free or paid ISBNs for the book. Some publishers such as kindle create and draft2digital provide a free ISBN, but it is valid only with that publisher. Other publishers provide the option of buying ISBNs for an additional price.

For Indian authors, Raja Rammohun Roy National Agency for ISBN https://isbn.gov.in/ is the agency where one can get a free ISBN by entering the book and author details. One must note that the approval process to get an ISBN in India can take a week or so. However, the process is free for authors and gives them the flexibility of having an ISBN that is not tied to a specific publisher like Amazon.

4.9 Conclusion

Publishing your e-book broadens your audience reach significantly. In this chapter, we detailed various platforms and strategies for authors to publish their e-books. In the following chapter, we consider the tangible aspect of your work—publishing a paperback edition.

Chapter 5: How to publish paperbacks

Although e-books are widely popular, many readers prefer physical books. This chapter guides you through the process of publishing paperbacks and hardcover books, including crucial decisions about design, binding, and distribution channels, particularly in India.

5.1 Additional options to select for designing paperback books

When designing a paperback or hardcover book, the authors have to fill in a few additional options related to the binding of the book and paper used for printing, such as the following:

- Black and white or color book (in case there are color pictures in the book and the author wishes them to appear with color)
- White paper or cream-colored paper
- Binding type (saddle stitch, soft cover, hard cover)
- Glossy or matte finish for the cover
- Size of the book (such as A4 or A5 or 5*7 inches, 6*9 inches)

The above choices also influence the price of the final book.

In setting the price, the online publishers set a minimum price for printing the book, based on the choices above. The author then has the option of setting a price larger than the minimum as they may see fit. The author royalties per book sold often depend on the margin over the minimum price which they have chosen.

For a hardcover book, there is usually a minimum number of pages needed to justify the minimum width of the spine.

5.2 Amazon Kindle Direct Publishing (KDP)

KDP (https://kdp.amazon.com/en_US/) can be used to publish print books as well as e-books, which will then be available for sale through Amazon.

However, the number of languages in which print books can be published using KDP is limited. For instance, it currently supports only the following four Indian languages:

- Hindi
- Tamil
- Marathi
- Malayalam

It does not cover other widely spoken languages such as Oriya, Bangla, Kannada etc. It is possible that the number of supported languages will expand in the future. Also, KDP does not allow for creating of paperbacks in the four Indian languages mentioned above, and only E-books are allowed.

5.3 IngramSpark

As mentioned in the previous chapter on eBooks, IngramSpark is a popular publisher for paperback and hardback books targeted to bookstores mainly in the US but also in countries like UK and Australia. They charge a fixed price for each book uploaded on their system, usually $49 with options for print book + ebook, $49 for print book only and $25 for ebook only. The author can use their web tools for designing the book. Therefore, adding a new book at IngramSpark is not free.

However, IngramSpark have a better range of publishers who stock books from them. The author has a choice of opting to allow returns of unsold books, which increases the costs for the author but also increases the chances of the book getting bought by potential bookstores. They do not provide an ISBN, however, to non-US authors. Only US authors get a free ISBN number. Non-US authors have to procure the ISBN from other sources.

5.4 Notion Press publishing (India specific)

Notion Press (https://notionpress.com/en) is quite a good site for publishing print books in India. It is one of the biggest self-publishing houses in India with a huge number of already published books. It has support for multiple Indian languages.

The services on the NotionPress website start from free, if the author wishes to use the online tools on the Notionpress website and publish the books without any expert assistance.

The minimum price at which the book is to be sold is set based on the number of pages and the size of the book and other features.

Using the online tools on the Notionpress website, the author has to select basic details of the books such as name, description, language, about the authors, page design and then upload the PDF of the ebook. It then goes through a seven day manual vetting process before the book is approved for publishing.

Alternatively, the authors can use the online tool available to copy and paste the text and images of the book into the template available on the NotionPress website. This process only takes two days.

Once the book is approved, NotionPress markets and sells the books on its own website and also to major retailers such as Amazon and Flipkart in India. In certain cases, it can also market the books internationally including to the US site of amazon.com and other places.

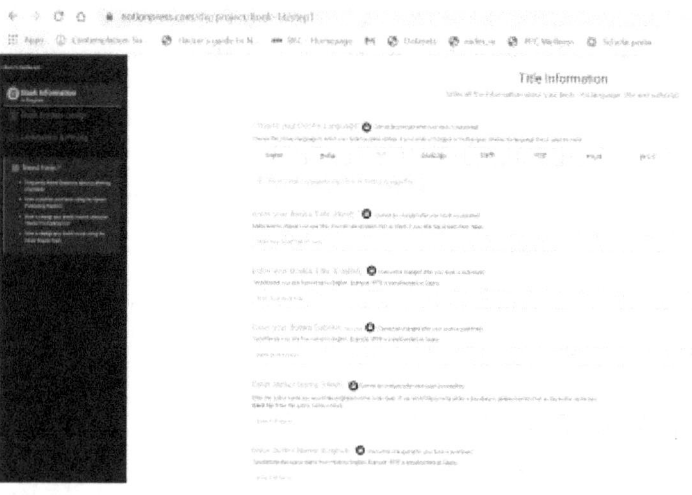

Figure: Interface of the Notion Press website for adding details of a new book

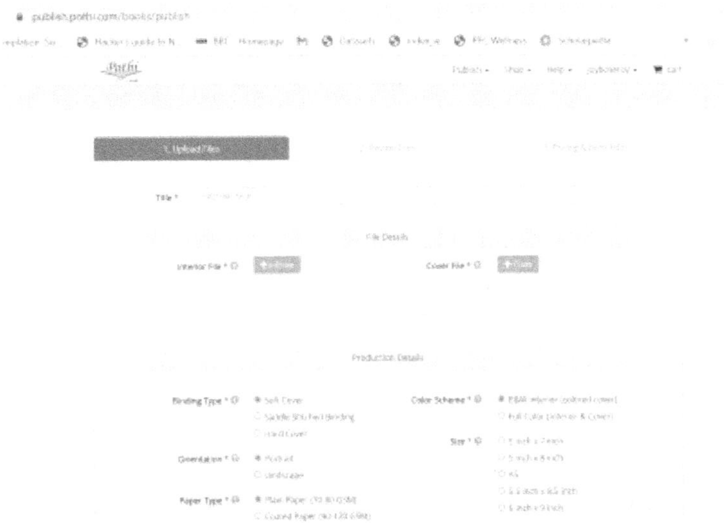

Figure: Interface of the Pothi.com website for adding details of a new book

5.5 Pothi.com (India specific)

Pothi (https://pothi.com/) is another site which is good for self-publishing using Print on Demand. Print on Demand refers to the case where the books are printed only if they are paid for and bought. This can be useful, for example, when the number of copies of the book are low and one wants to distribute early copies of the book among their friends and select readers. The pothi.com interface is very easy to use and intuitive. They have the facility to create both paper editions as well as PDF editions of the books. Using it can be free or the author can pay for additional services such as editing, proofreading and design.

Pothi.com also supports multiple Indian languages.

5.6 Other Indian self-publishing sites

There are also quite a good number of other Indian sites for publishing one's printed books, each having their own pros and cons. One can search on google or quora for a more exhaustive list.

Some of them include the following (most of them offer both paperback and e-book publishing):

- White Falcon Publishing https://whitefalconpublishing.com/
- Blue Rose Publishers https://bluerosepublishers.com/
- 24by7 publishing https://www.24by7publishing.com/
- Blue Hill publications https://bluehillpublications.in/
- Become Shakespeare https://www.becomeshakespeare.com/
- Partridge Publishing https://www.partridgepublishing.com/en-in
- Evincepub https://evincepub.com/
- BookLeaf Publishing https://www.bookleafpub.com/ : BookLeaf offers a

100% royalty model, allowing authors to keep all proceeds from their book sales. They support both paperback and eBook formats and provide global distribution.

- Clever Fox Publishing https://cleverfoxpublishing.com/ : One of India's fastest-growing hybrid publishers, with offices in Chennai, Bangalore, and London. Publishing packages start from ₹2,500 and include an AI-powered Author Dashboard for sales tracking and royalty monitoring. Books are distributed across 40,000+ stores worldwide.
- IndiePress https://indiepress.in/ : Based in Bangalore, IndiePress offers a streamlined 30-day publishing process including cover design, editing, printing, marketing, and book launches. They have published over 30,000 authors and aim to help authors reach a broad audience.
- Zorba Books https://www.zorbabooks.com/ : A well-regarded Indian self-publishing platform providing editorial, design, distribution, and marketing services. They have a strong focus on helping debut Indian authors navigate the publishing process with transparency and affordability.

5.7 Conclusion

In this chapter, we have discussed various websites for authors to publish their paperback books and hardcovers in India, in various Indian languages and in English. We went through the nuances of paperback publication, from choosing paper types to distribution options specific to India. In the next chapter, we delve into the rapidly growing market of audiobooks, another excellent format to expand your reader base.

Chapter 6: How to Publish Audiobooks

Nowadays, audio books are becoming more and more popular and their sales are increasing every year. Many people like to listen to audio books while working out, jogging, commuting, driving or even before sleeping. Many people may, in fact, prefer audio books to printed books or e-books.

Many published authors may wish to re-publish their existing published book as an audio book. They can be used as an additional means for authors to reach a wider audience. An author may also wish to directly publish their manuscript in audio book form instead of first getting a print edition and audio edition. They may also want to convert an existing podcast or YouTube video series into an audio book.

In this chapter, we cover everything from recording techniques to distribution, enabling you to capitalize on this growing trend. We focus on what is available specifically for Indian authors to enable them to publish their audio books.

To produce an audio book, one needs to record the book chapters professionally and design a proper cover image for the book.

In the following sections, we describe the steps to publish an audio book.

6.1 Preparing audio files of book narration

The author has to first prepare the audio files for their audiobook. These can be in MP3 or other common formats.

One way for authors to prepare the audio files is to narrate and record the narration of the book by themselves. This needs to be done with professional equipment including a good audio recorder or software, a good headphone and speakers and the recording should be done in a quiet room.

The authors should take care to speak slowly with a clear voice, and annotate their voices as per the situation described in the particular chapter of their audiobook. For fiction books, narration for different characters should be done differently.

The authors need to save each section or each chapter of the book as a separate audio file. Therefore, the title, preface and other sections, and each chapter should be separately recorded and saved as separate MP3 files. It is helpful to name the files in a relevant and meaningful way such as Preface.mp3, Chapter1.mp3, Table of Contents.mp3 and so on.

The other option for authors, instead of recording the audio book by themselves, is to hire a good narrator with a clear voice who can agree to narrate for their audio book. The fees for professional narrators can either be fixed or negotiable, based on criteria such as the time in hours for reading the audio book and the number of words in the book.

It is better to find a professional narrator with previous experience of making audio books and ideally they should be a native English speaker (or native speaker of whichever language the book is written in).

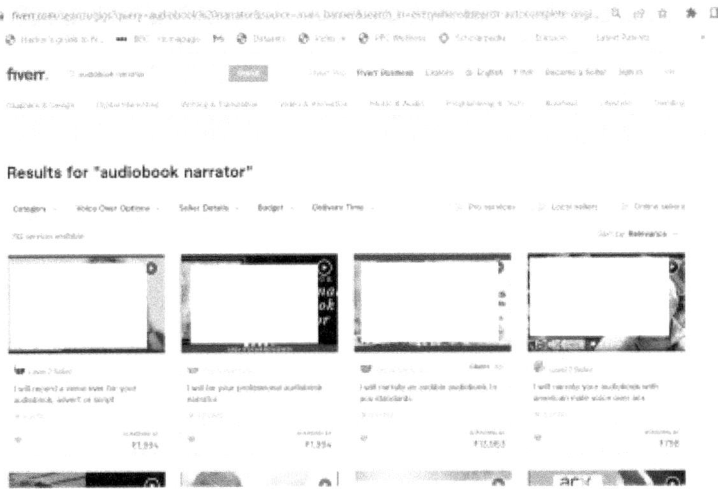

Figure: Using fiverr.com to search for professional audiobook narrators

Some good places to find a professional narrator for hire include the following:

- ACX by Amazon (ACX is currently limited to only a few countries, and its books are published in amazon's audible among others) https://www.acx.com/
- Findaway voices https://findawayvoices.com/
- Freelance gig sites like Fiverr (https://www.fiverr.com/) or Upwork.com.

One problem currently with ACX and audible is that they don't directly support Indian authors and books published from India. One way around this problem is to get a friend to publish the book from the US or UK.

Alternatively, an Indian author can publish their recorded audiobook using sites like Findaway Voices who will distribute the audiobooks to Audible along with other audiobook sellers like Kobo and apple.

It is important to remember that audible and other audiobook sellers have strict guidelines for audiobooks, related to the voice quality, background noise, speed and clarity and so on. It is important to make sure the recorded audio files meet these guidelines. Professional narrators or people with previous experience in narrating audio books are preferable for this reason.

6.2 AI enabled auto-narrated audio books at Google Play

Google Play has recently launched a feature named auto narrated audiobooks. Using this, authors can simply upload the EPUB files of their books and choose settings such as voice, accent etc of the AI enabled speaker. Google will generate an audiobook based on the reading of the book using a synthesized voice.

This feature is made possible using state of the art Artificial Intelligence (AI) technologies including natural language processing (NLP), text to speech (TTS) and speech processing. The results look very realistic, although still not as genuine as a human voice. Things such as intonations are still better spoken by a human.

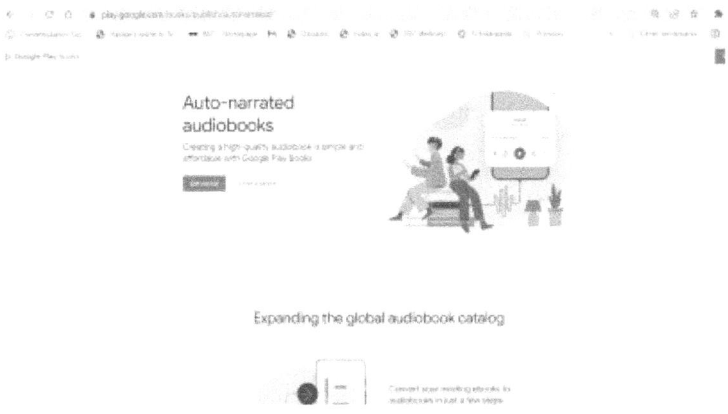

Figure: Front page for auto narrated audiobooks

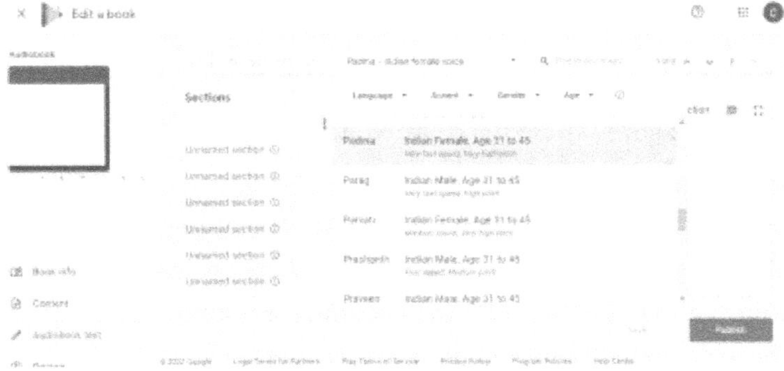

Figure: Interface to choose the type of voice and accent in Google play auto-narrated audiobooks

The author can select the narration in a choice of accents, pitch and speed.

This feature, however, is only available for users in a few selected countries at the moment, including USA, UK, Canada, Australia and New Zealand. Users in other countries will need to wait for now.

Such auto narrated audio books provide a much cheaper and convenient alternative for authors to either narrating the book by themselves or finding a professional human speaker to narrate the books for them.

However, currently having books with synthetic narration is not accepted in most of the audiobook stores such as Amazon's audible or audio books at Apple. Only a few publishers such as Kobo allow authors to upload auto narrated audiobooks.

The URL is https://play.google.com/books/publish/autonarrated/

6.3 Designing a cover image for the audio book

Once the audio files are recorded, the next step for an author is to design a cover image for the audio book. The cover image should ideally be shaped as a square, and consists of a cover image, title of the book and name of the authors. There are some guidelines related to the minimum resolution and size of the cover image, which should be adhered to.

Here again, one can use a website such as canva.com to design the cover of the audiobook, similar to the tools and websites described for e-books and paperbacks in the previous chapters.

6.4 Submission of the audio book

Once the audio files are ready and cover is created, the author may submit them to any of the audio book sites for distribution and sales.

Sites like ACX and Findaway voices may have their own stringent rules for deciding whether to accept the book for distribution.

Usually if the author gets the narration done by a professional narrator with experience, they should be fine. For amazon audible, it is better to have the print book and/or e-book (with the same title and authors) also published on amazon.com.

The author also has to set a price for the audio book and a library price for lending to libraries. There is a guidance for the price which varies with the length of the audio book in hours. The author can view the prices at which other audio books of the same genre and length are being sold before deciding upon the appropriate price to sell their audio books.

6.5 Approval for sale

Once the audio book files and cover image pass the quality checks of the distribution site, it will then be approved for sale on the site (such as findawayvoices.com or ACX.com) or distributed to various audio book sites including Audible.

6.6 Promoting the audiobooks

For authors, it is important to try and work hard to promote the audio books as widely as possible. It is good to promote the book in different channels and with different groups of people such as friends and reading groups. One may also have book readings, podcasts, attend book festivals and conventions, write blogs and so on to promote the book and reach the potential buyers.

Publishing an audio book takes a lot of hard work, no doubt. But it is equally rewarding to get it finally published and available for people to buy and listen to.

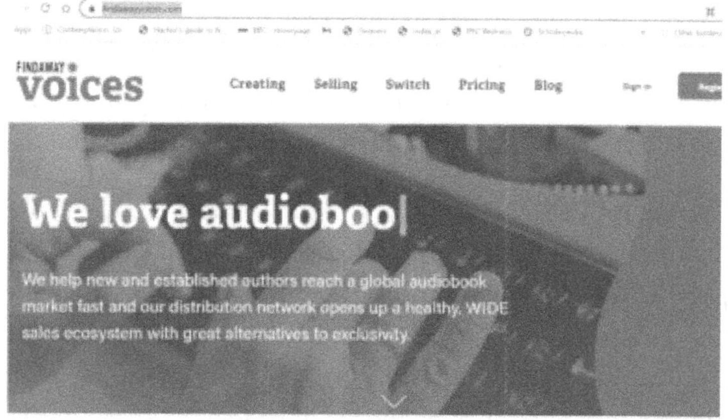

Figure: Website of Findaway voices, a popular site for creating audiobooks

In the following subsections, we look at a few popular publishers for publishing and distributing audio books.

6.7 Findaway Voices

Findaway voices is a good site both for finding the professional narrators to narrate and record the audio book, as well as to send the approved book to different distributors including google play audiobooks and amazon's audible.

Given that Amazon's ACX is currently only available in select countries, it might be the only way for authors from countries like India to put their recorded audio books on audible.com.

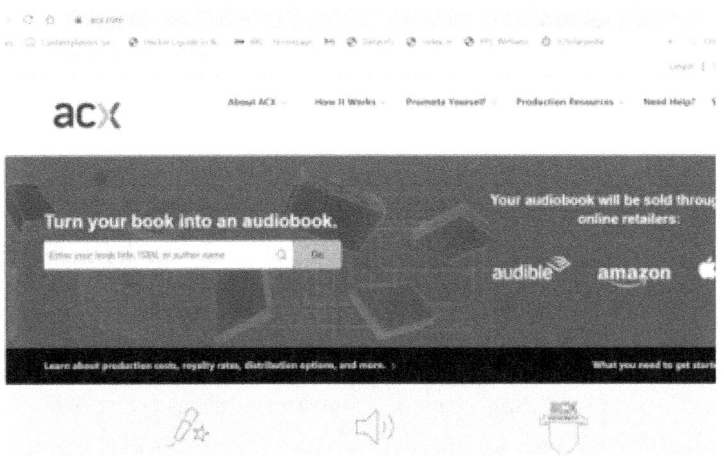

Figure: Website of ACX, good for creating audiobooks content on audible.com

6.8 ACX

Amazon's ACX is the most popular site for authors to put their books on amazon's audible (www.audible.com), where they can be bought by the customers of Amazon audible, which is by far the largest market for audiobooks currently.

It can also help connect the author to readers and narrators who can record the audiobook professionally and at a reasonable price depending on the length of the book.

However, ACX is currently only available directly for authors in select countries, notable USA and UK. Authors in other countries like India can use other means like Findaway voices.

6.9 Conclusion

In this chapter, we covered essential steps for producing and distributing audiobooks, offering you a new dimension to engage readers who prefer listening. As we can see, the options for an author in India to publish audiobooks are somewhat limited, since they cannot use auto narrated audiobooks or ACX.

The primary method available is to hire a professional audio book narrator using freelance websites such as fiverr.com or upwork.com and get them to record the audio files for the book.

Once the audio files for the book are recorded professionally, an Indian author can use Findaway voices to distribute the audiobook to various retailers including Audible, Kobo, Barnes and Noble and others.

In the next chapter, we address the specifics of publishing books in Indian languages to help you reach even more readers.

Chapter 7: Publishing Indian language books

Publishing in Indian regional languages can significantly broaden your readership. In this chapter, we tackle the unique challenges and solutions for effectively publishing books in various Indian languages, ensuring you tap into this valuable market. We focus on support and options available for Indian language books on Kindle and other publishing mediums.

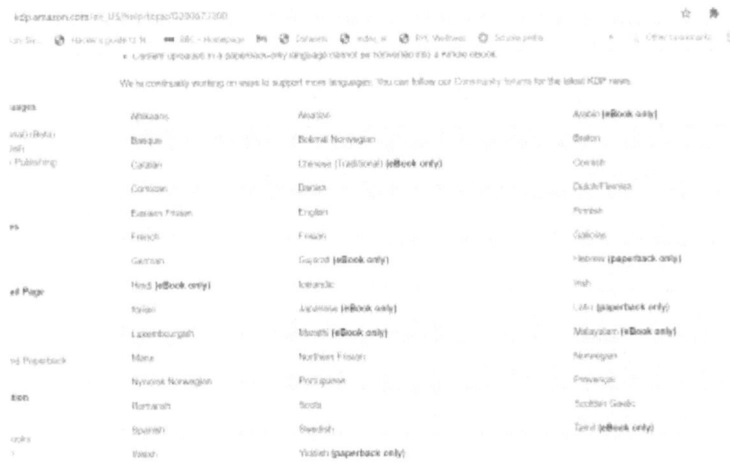

Figure: List of supported languages shown on Amazon KDP website

7.1 Languages currently supported on Amazon KDP

Currently, Amazon kindle KDP supports only the following Indian languages: Hindi, Marathi, Tamil and Malayalam.

Other Indian languages like Bengali or Gujarati are still not supported on kindle KDP, although ebooks in these other languages can be submitted by established publishers for sale on amazon. Therefore, one can only write Kindle E-books in the four supported Indian languages at present.

Even these four Indian languages are only supported for self-publishing e-books on Kindle using KDP (Kindle Direct Publishing) and not paperbacks or hardbacks. Therefore, the Indian authors would have to create the paperback editions for their books using a third-party Indian book publisher such as Notionpress or Pothi.com.

Draft2Digital has also recently started the facility for creating paperback editions in various languages. However, here too currently the paperbacks are not supported in the Indian languages, possibly because of concerns about widespread availability of Indian language fonts and a sufficient readership market for books in Indian languages.

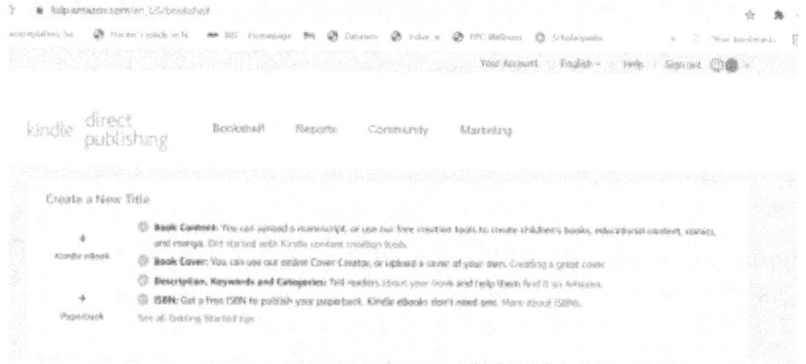

Figure: The Amazon KDP interface for adding a new book

7.2 Procedure for self-publishing in KDP supported Indian languages

For KDP supported languages (Hindi, Marathi, Tamil and Malayalam) the procedure for publishing a book is as follows:

- Write the book manuscript using a word editing software such as Microsoft word
- Or else, download the kindle create software from the link and edit the book there
- Or else, create the book in a format that most e-readers (such as nook and apple books) understand: such as EPUB. Google for how to create a book in EPUB format.
- Go to Amazon KDP website https://kdp.amazon.com/en_US/
- Sign in, click the icon for "+Kindle e-book"
- Choose the language, fill in metadata details such as title, summary and keywords
- In the next page after entering metadata details, upload the manuscript of the Indian language book as a MS Word file or Amazon kindle format file KPF, or EPUB.
- Design a cover for the e-book. Here the author can either use Amazon cover creator, which is easy to use, or upload their own image of the cover.
- Preview all the content for the finished book.
- Set the pricing levels. For amazon.in, the minimum price can for buying the e-book be Rupees 49 for India market. However, an author can enroll their book in KDP Select and then the book becomes part of

Kindle unlimited and free to kindle unlimited subscribers. Books in KDP select can also be submitted for special offers such as free or discounted for a limited time.

It must be noted here that KDP select contract is exclusive, so an author cannot submit the KDP sekect enrolled E-book to other publishers such as Google play books or Barnes and Noble, for the length of time it is enrolled in KDP select.

7.3 Non-KDP options for self-publishing Indian language books

If an author has to publish their book in an Indian language other than the KDP supported ones, the options are as described below.

- Publish the book on other platforms than kindle KDP. Choices of such platforms include Kobo, Google play books, Apple books, and so on. For google play books, one can publish them in Google play partner center. For other platforms one can use a site such as draft2digital and publish their Indian language book there. Draft2digital can distribute the book to other platforms free of charge: one just needs to set up the tax data and other details on the website.
- Publish the book on Indian self-publishing sites such as Notion Press and Pothi. Pothi supports both e-books and paperbacks publishing, while Notion press mainly supports paperbacks at the moment. Therefore, in pothi, one can publish the Indian

language book as a PDF and set up an appropriate price for selling the PDF e-book.

- There are many other third-party sites and apps for Indian e-books self-publishing. One can search on google to get some sites for the same. An example is Pratilipi (https://pratilipi.com/), one of India's largest platforms for Indian language books, which supports over twelve Indian languages including Hindi, Marathi, Gujarati, Bengali, Tamil, Telugu, Kannada, and Malayalam. Authors can publish stories, novels, and poetry on Pratilipi and build a dedicated readership. Matrubharti (https://matrubharti.com/) is another Indian platform specifically focused on regional language content, particularly Gujarati, Hindi, Marathi, and others. The Pencil app also supports a number of Indian languages.
- One can use the conventional publishing sites for Indian language books (not self-publishing). However, this is a longer process and needs vetting of the book by the publishers, as mentioned in chapter 1.

7.4 Conclusion

In this chapter, we have presented a short outline of the steps for Indian authors to publish their Indian language e-books in amazon kindle and other options. After the Indian language book or ebook is published, authors must also pay attention to marketing the published book via various channels, as well as promoting your book to ensure it reaches the right audience.

Chapter 8: Marketing and promoting the books

Your publishing journey does not end once your book is available. Effective marketing is critical for success. This chapter offers practical strategies and insights on promoting your books to reach your target audience effectively and sustainably.

8.1 Free or discounted e-book promotions

Amazon KDP Select is one mechanism by which authors can promote their e-books by making them part of Kindle unlimited and also running free or discounted book promotions. However, KDP select is exclusive in nature, meaning the authors have to agree not to list their e-books for sale on any other e-book sites other than Amazon.

Free and discounted e-book promotions are likewise also available with other e-book publishers such as Draft2Digital, Google play books, Kobo, Notion Press and so on.

8.2 Attending book events

Another way for self-published authors to promote their books and e-books include attending events such as book festivals, book fairs, book readings, and book signings. However, for this building a good network of other authors and publishers is important, since some of these events are based on invitation only.

8.3 Publishing blog posts, videos and podcasts

The authors can promote themselves and their books by having a blog which they update regularly. They can also put YouTube or vimeo videos of book readings and discussions related to the book. They can also release podcasts of discussions on topics related to the published books.

Over time, these activities have a cumulative effect and result in a steady growth of readers. But it takes hard work and one should never expect overnight results.

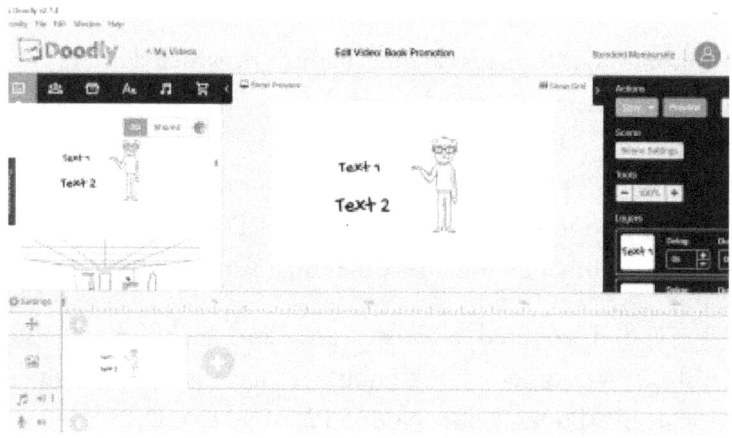

Figure: Doodly software to make video animations to promote one's book

8.4 Using Video Animations to Promote the Book

An author can also make video animations to promote their book.

It is very easy nowadays to make animations using cheap and widely available software such as doodly (https://www.doodly.com/) and doodle maker (https://doodlemaker.com/go/).

These animated videos can include voiceovers. Once made, such videos can be uploaded to the author's website, the amazon.com author page and other online portals to promote the book.

8.5 Dedicated author website and book website

Another way for authors to promote their books is to build a professional looking website for themselves and their books. Wordpress.com is a good site to create professional looking websites with minimal effort.

Ideally one should get a domain registered in their name. However this is not always needed and the Wordpress site is sufficient as long as it can be discovered by search engines such as google. One can buy a domain name for reasonably cheap prices from websites such as godaddy.com, wix.com or even from wordpress.

Sometimes, especially in case of academic and non-fiction books, the authors can put additional resources on each of the book websites, that interested readers can come and check.

8.6 Using social media to promote the books

Social networking sites such as Instagram, facebook, twitter, pinterest, tiktok, quora, linkedIn and other social media websites can be used by authors to promote their books as well.

For facebook, the author can make a facebook page with details of all their books.

For twitter, the author can tweet about their upcoming books, special discounts, extracts and articles from the books and so on. It is good to include more images in the tweets, as they help to attract the reader's attention. Knowing which hashtags to use in the tweets to reach a wider audience is also an important skill.

Quora can be used by authors to establish themselves in the field by answering questions related to the topic of their books, and also by making a dedicated space to share their articles.

Instagram is good for reaching a wide audience quickly, however the authors should take care to focus their Instagram feed purely on their books, and publish book extracts, saying, pictures from book signings, videos of book readings and so on. Here too, the choice of good images and properly selected hashtags is important.

LinkedIn is good for authors to make professional connections with other authors and book publishers.

Pinterest is good for making pins of extracts from the author's books, in a good design that people can share widely.

8.7 Offering teasers and book extracts for free download

The authors can also put book extracts for free download, to increase interest and curiosity towards the books in their prospective readers. These can be provided through the author's websites or through social media.

Extracts of the books can be included with the sales channels as well. For example, Amazon kindle typically display the first few pages of the kindle ebooks for prospective readers to browse before deciding to buy the books.

Figure: Amazon author page for JK Rowling

8.8 Using the Amazon author page

The Amazon author page https://author.amazon.com/ is another way for authors to promote themselves. It allows the authors of books listed on amazon to provide information about themselves in multiple languages, along with uploading pictures and videos related to the published books.

8.9 Using Goodreads

Goodreads website (goodreads.com) is a popular website for book reviewers and hence can be another way for authors to promote their books.

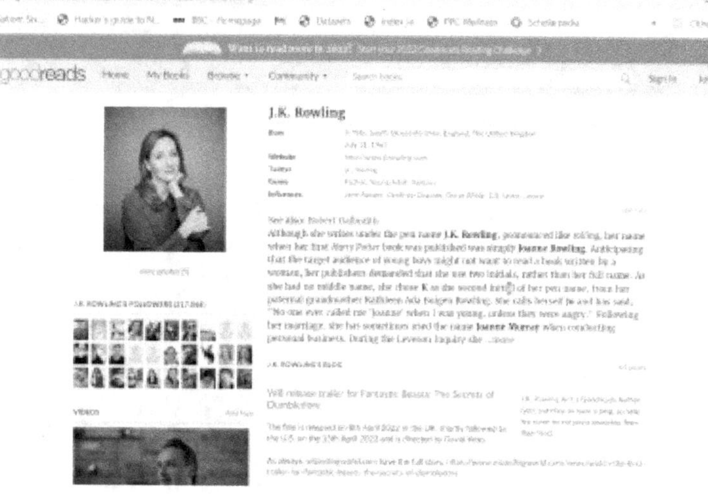

Figure: Goodreads author page for JK Rowling

The first step is to get approved as a published author on goodreads. Once that is done, the goodreads authors can add details of various books, extracts from the books, sayings and videos related to the published books and so on. Readers can also leave their reviews for the books on the goodreads author webpage.

8.10 Using Google and Facebook ads

Authors can also use google ads (https://ads.google.com/intl/en_IN/home/) and facebook ads (https://www.facebook.com/business/ads) to promote their books.

Even amazon has started an ads program (https://advertising.amazon.com/help) where on putting specific keywords the author's books can appear on top of the search list.

For all these the payment is on a per click basis. The authors can put a budget to be spent each day. Once the daily budget is met, no more ads will be shown for that day.

8.11 BookTok and Short-Form Video Marketing

One of the most significant and relatively recent developments in book marketing is the rise of BookTok — a vibrant community of book lovers and authors on TikTok who share book reviews, recommendations, and author content in short-form videos. As of 2025, the #BookTok hashtag has accumulated over 370 billion views on TikTok. Authors who have embraced BookTok have seen dramatic increases in book sales, and several previously overlooked books have become bestsellers through this channel alone.

For Indian authors, TikTok may have varying availability depending on the region and device. However, Instagram Reels and YouTube Shorts offer very similar short-form video capabilities and reach enormous audiences in India. Authors can create short videos showing their writing process, sharing quotes and extracts from their books, doing book unboxings, responding to reader questions, or discussing themes from their books. Authenticity and consistency are key — audiences respond well to authors who share genuine insights into their writing journey rather than purely promotional content.

8.12 Building an Email Newsletter

Data consistently shows that email marketing is among the most effective tools for authors to connect with readers and drive book sales. An email newsletter allows authors to communicate directly with readers who have already expressed interest in their work, without relying on any social media platform's algorithms. Authors earning substantial incomes from self-publishing typically maintain email subscriber lists running into the thousands.

Authors can use free or low-cost email marketing platforms such as Mailchimp (https://mailchimp.com/), Substack (https://substack.com/), or ConvertKit (https://convertkit.com/) to build and manage their mailing lists. A common strategy is to offer a free chapter, short story, or related resource as an incentive for readers to sign up for the newsletter. Once subscribed, readers can be regularly updated about new book releases, promotions, behind-the-scenes content, and upcoming events. This builds a loyal readership that an author can rely on for every new book launch.

8.13 Conclusion

To conclude, writing and publishing a book is only the first step for self-published authors. Marketing is equally important to reach a wider audience, who can be potential buyers for the books.

Marketing their books is hard work for self-published authors and must be done over a sustained period of time to get good results. However, it is also quite rewarding and can get a wider audience to read and become aware of the books.

We explored various effective marketing strategies to enhance visibility and sales, crucial for the success of self-published authors. Finally, we will summarize the entire journey and key takeaways in the concluding chapter.

Chapter 9: Conclusion

In this book, we have discussed various tools and techniques that authors in India can use to self-publish their books. We have included E-books, audio books and paperbacks. We have also discussed how AI writing tools such as ChatGPT, Google Gemini, and Claude can assist authors during the writing process, and covered new marketing channels including BookTok, Instagram Reels, and email newsletters that have become increasingly important for self-published authors. We have also included a wider range of Indian self-publishing platforms that have emerged or grown in recent years, including Clever Fox Publishing, BookLeaf, IndiePress, and Zorba Books, among others.

We have covered various strategies that authors can use for writing, publishing and marketing the self-published books. We have also covered books in Indian languages and India-based publishers of books.

It is not an easy job for a self-published author to publish their books and also sell them widely. The competition is quite fierce in the self-publishing market. It needs many months or even years of sustained efforts in promoting the books, writing multiple books and having supplementary activities such as blogs and podcasts. It is a good idea for authors to be realistic about the prospects for their new book, and be ready to do the hard work of promoting the book using every possible means.

However, if the author is ready to do the needed hard work and provide value for their readers, their efforts can bear fruit over time and self-published books can even become bestsellers.

About the Authors

Siva Prasad Bose has authored more than twenty introductory guidebooks related to aspects of Indian laws in Hindi and English. He is currently retired after many years of service in Uttar Pradesh Power Corporation Limited. He received his engineering degree from Jadavpur University, Kolkata, has a law degree from Meerut University, Meerut and Bachelor of Science degree from MMH College in Ghaziabad. His interests lie in the fields of family law, civil law, law of contracts, and areas of law related to electricity generation and revenue related issues.

Joy Bose is a researcher and a data scientist.

Other Books by Siva Prasad Bose

Introduction to Wills and Probate

Senior Citizens Abuse in India

Introduction to Negotiable Instruments

Introduction to Marriage Laws in India

Neighbor Problems in India and what to do about them

Managing Court Cases with Mental Strength

Delays in Court Cases in India

Introduction to Patents and Patent Law in India

Introduction to Property Law in India

Did you love *Self Publish Books and e-Books in India*? Then you should read *A Walk in Chittaranjan Park*[1] by Siva Prasad Bose and Joy Bose!

[2]

Chittaranjan Park or CR park is a residential colony in South Delhi, bordered by Greater Kailash 1 and 2 and located close to areas such as Nehru place, Alaknanda, Kalkaji and Govindpuri. It is sometimes called "Little Kolkata" because of the Kolkata style street food, Bengali culture and festivals celebrated here.

Previously called EPDP Colony or East Pakistan Displaced Persons Colony and Purbachal, CR Park is a Bengali dominated colony that was originally developed to house

---

1. https://books2read.com/u/bMYWXv

2. https://books2read.com/u/bMYWXv

refugees of partition from East Bengal, but has recently become more diverse. It is a cultural treat famous for its celebration of Durga Puja, Bengali snacks and sweets.

In this book we discuss the famous landmarks and festivals in CR Park. This is intended to be partly a travel guide for those who want to experience this microcosm of Bengali culture in New Delhi.

Our own Bose family has been resident in Delhi for a very long time, originally residing in Kashmere Gate and later moving to CR Park.

About the Author

Siva Prasad Bose is an electrical engineer by profession. He is currently retired after many years of service in Uttar Pradesh Power Corporation Limited. He received his engineering degree from Jadavpur University, Kolkata and has a law degree from Meerut University, Meerut. His interests lie in the fields of family law, civil law, law of contracts, and any areas of law related to power electricity related issues.

Read more at https://sivaprasadbose.wordpress.com/.

www.ingramcontent.com/pod-product-compliance
Lightning Source LLC
Chambersburg PA
CBHW052102150726
48002CB00002B/1000